SHIPS AHOY!
Hovercraft
by Kaitlyn Duling
BLASTOFF! 2 READERS
BLASTOFF! READERS, AN IMPRINT OF BELLWETHER MEDIA BY FLUTTERBEE

**Blastoff! Readers** are carefully developed by literacy experts to build reading stamina and move students toward fluency by combining standards-based content with developmentally appropriate text.

**Level 1** provides the most support through repetition of high-frequency words, light text, predictable sentence patterns, and strong visual support.

**Level 2** offers early readers a bit more challenge through varied sentences, increased text load, and text-supportive special features.

**Level 3** advances early-fluent readers toward fluency through increased text load, less reliance on photos, advancing concepts, longer sentences, and more complex special features.

★ **Blastoff! Universe**

Reading Level

Grade K

Grades 1–3

Blastoff! Discovery

Grade 4

This edition first published in 2026 by Bellwether Media, Inc.



For information regarding permission, write to Bellwether Media, Inc., Attention: Permissions Department, 3500 American Blvd W, Suite 150, Bloomington, MN 55431.

Library of Congress Cataloging-in-Publication Data is available at www.loc.gov or upon request from the publisher.

ISBN: 9798893048018 (hardcover)
ISBN: 9798893049015 (ebook)

Editor: Kieran Downs Designer: Jennifer Bowyer

Printed in the United States of America, North Mankato, MN.

# Table of Contents

# What Are Hovercraft?

Hovercraft are ships that use air to move.

Instead of sitting in the water, hovercraft float above it. They **hover**!

Hovercraft can be small or large. The **hull** is a rectangle with rounded corners.

## Parts of a Hovercraft

fans

Fans move hovercraft.
**Engines** power the fans.

**Lift** fans push air down into the ship's **skirt**. The skirt traps the air and helps the hovercraft float.

**Thrust** fans push the ship forward and backward.

## Types of Hovercraft

passenger hovercraft

military hovercraft

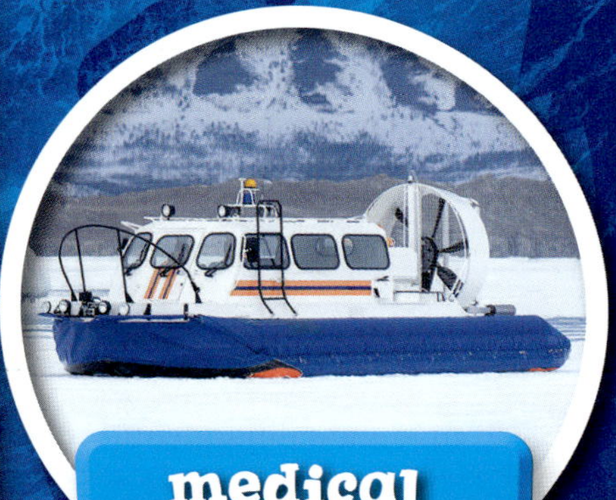

medical hovercraft

racing hovercraft

Passenger hovercraft move people. **Military** hovercraft move soldiers and supplies.

**Medical** hovercraft help people who are hurt. Racing hovercraft speed to the finish line!

# Floating Fun

Small hovercraft can be driven by one person. These can sometimes carry up to six passengers.

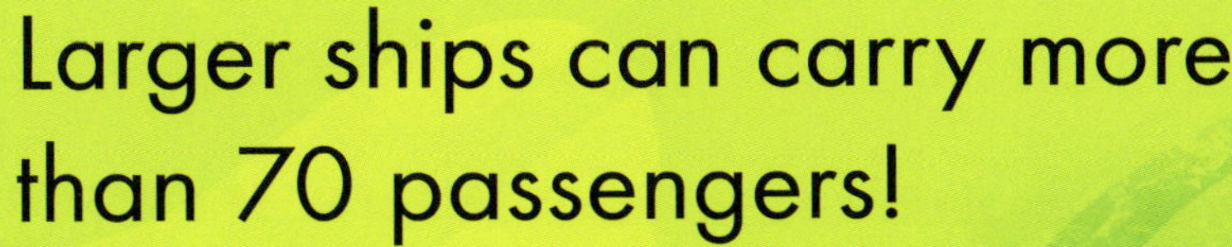

Larger ships can carry more than 70 passengers!

## Ship Stats

### Island Flyer

**Size** 77.2 feet (22 meters) long; 32.8 feet (10 meters) wide

**Type** passenger hovercraft

**Top Speed** 45 knots (51.8 miles or 83.3 kilometers per hour)

**Purpose** carries passengers between the Isle of Wight and Southsea in the United Kingdom

Hovercraft have **rudders**. The **pilot** uses them to turn the ship left and right.

## Hovercraft Movement

1 An engine sends power to the fans.

2 Lift fans blow air downward into the skirt, forming a cushion of air and creating lift.

3 Thrust fans blow air backward creating thrust.

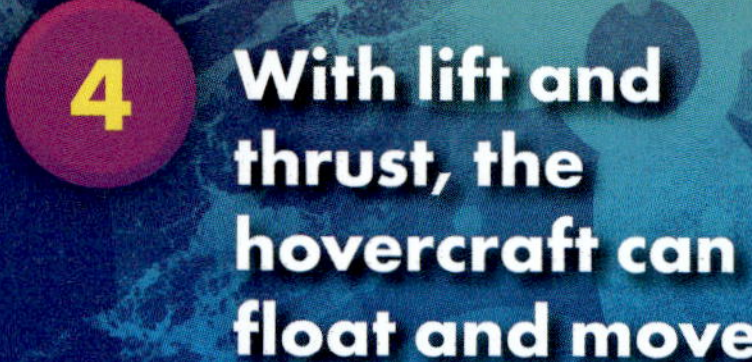

4 With lift and thrust, the hovercraft can float and move.

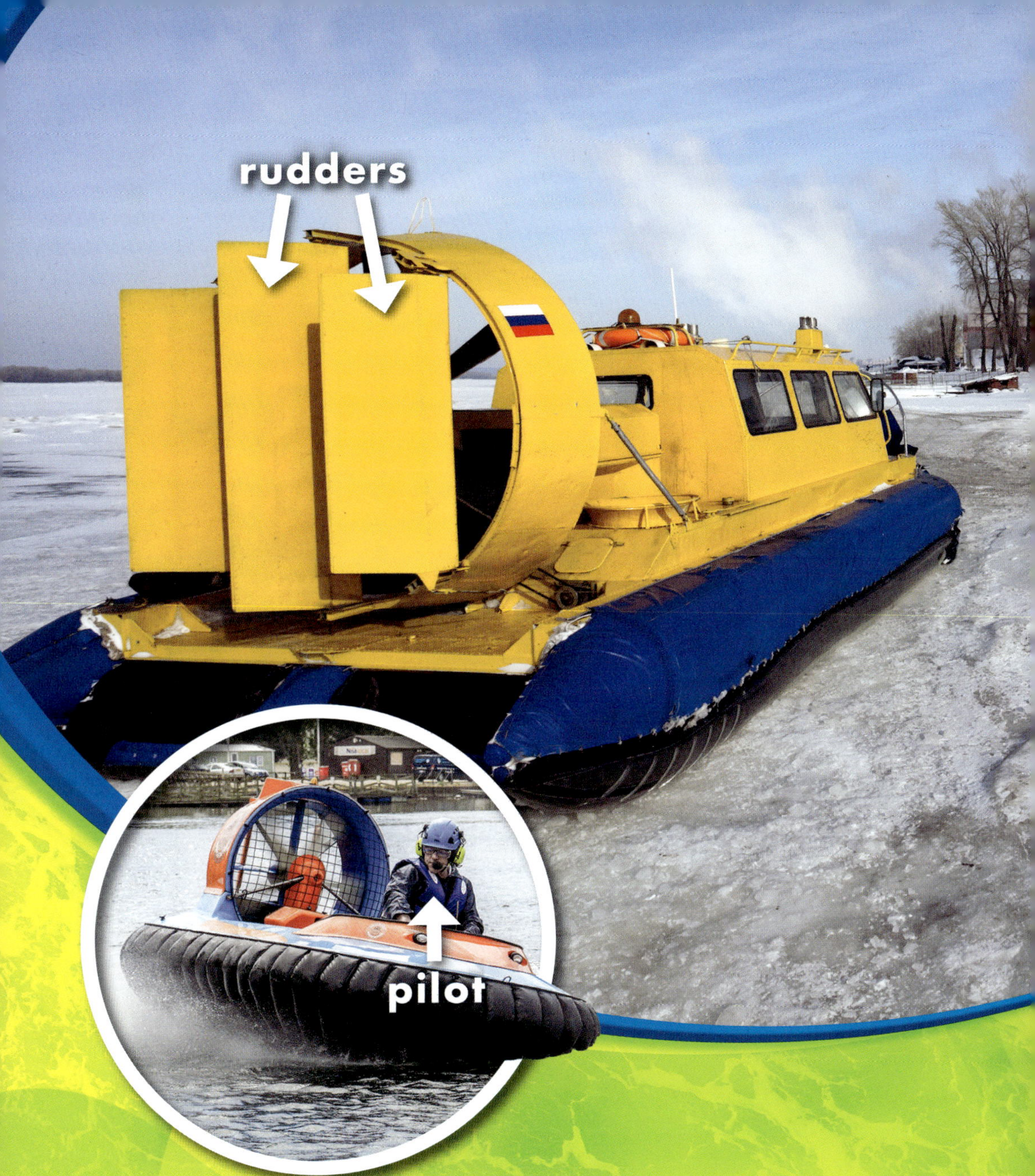

rudders

pilot

Pilots can also move their body to help turn small ships.

Hovercraft can move on water or land.

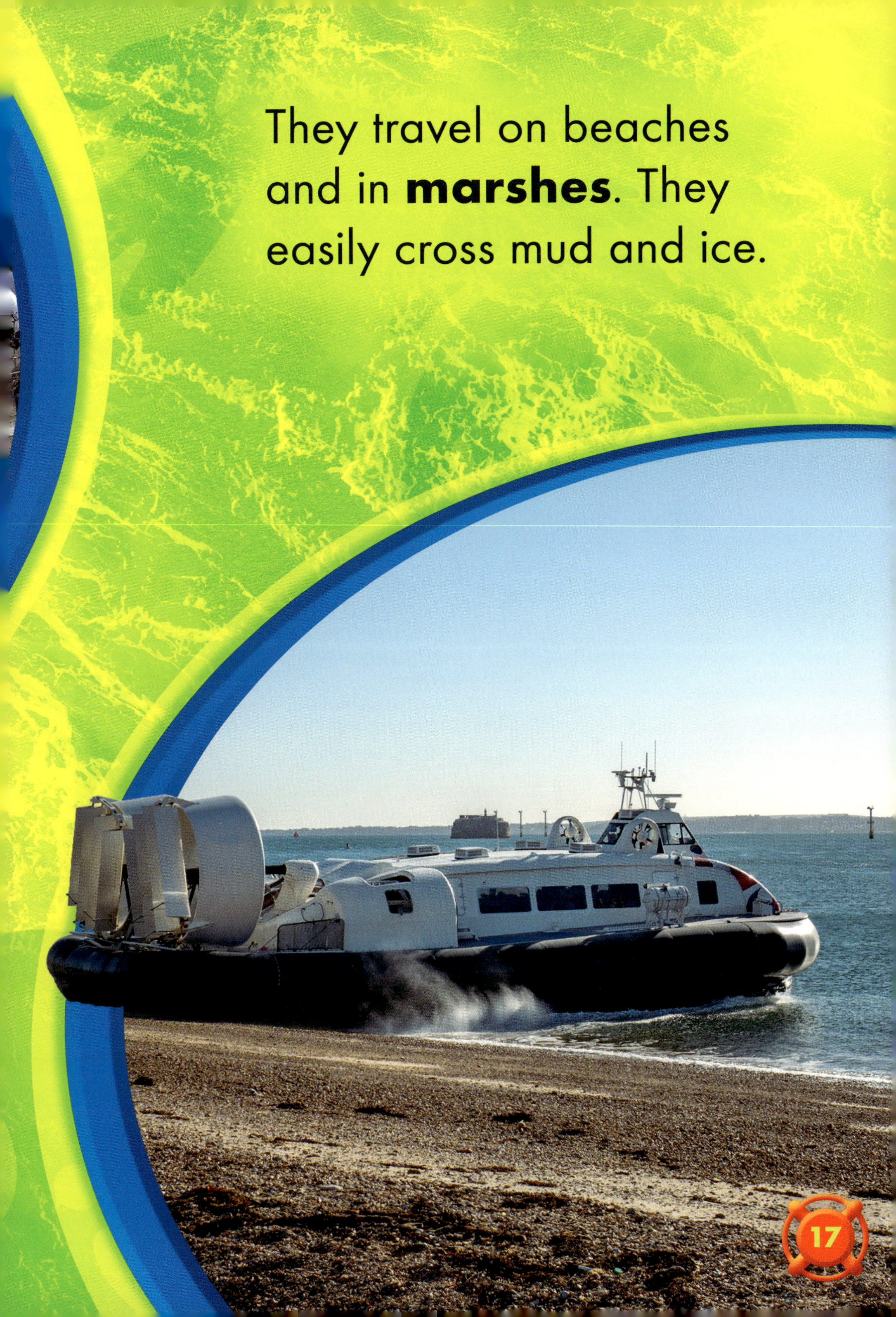

They travel on beaches and in **marshes**. They easily cross mud and ice.

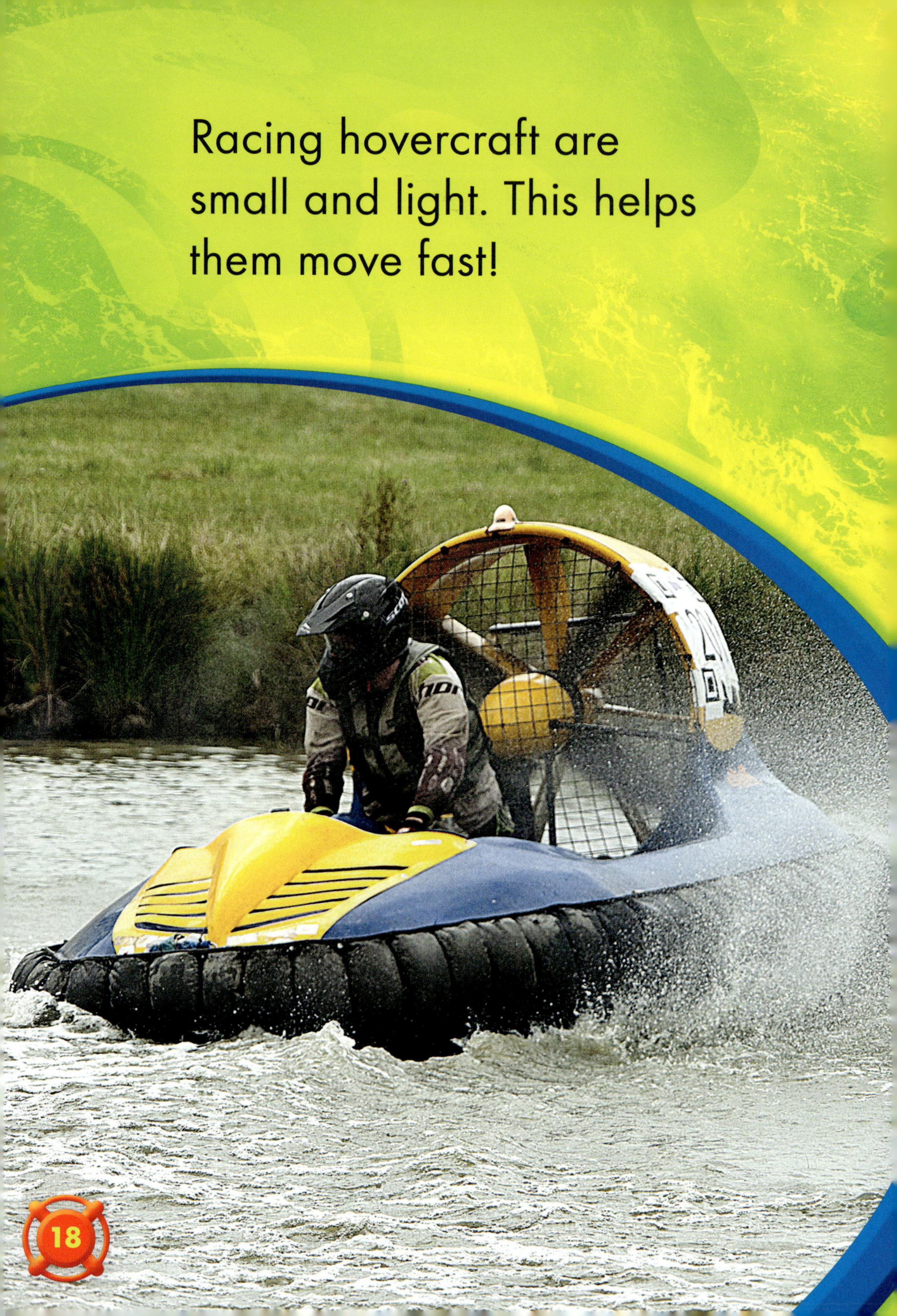

Racing hovercraft are small and light. This helps them move fast!

The fastest racing hovercraft can travel around 74 **knots** (85 miles or 137 kilometers per hour).

# Helpful Hovercraft

Hovercraft go where other ships cannot. They help during floods and other disasters.

They travel across snow, ice, sand, and mud. Helpful hovercraft get the job done!

# Glossary

**engines**—machines with moving parts that change power into motion

**hover**—to stay in one place in the air

**hull**—the main body of a ship

**knots**—units of measurement used to explain the speed of a ship

**lift**—the force that pushes something up

**marshes**—low, wet lands

**medical**—related to something used to help sick or injured people

**military**—related to the armed forces

**pilot**—people who drive hovercraft

**rudders**—flat pieces of wood or metal used to steer ships

**skirt**—a rubber barrier that surrounds the base of a hovercraft

**thrust**—the force that pushes something forward

# To Learn More

## AT THE LIBRARY

Miller, Marie-Therese. *Land and Water Combat Vehicles.* Minneapolis, Minn.: Lerner Publications, 2025.

Pang, Ursula. *Boats.* Buffalo, N.Y.: PowerKids Press, 2024.

Walker, Alan. *Ships Go!* New York, N.Y.: Crabtree Publishing Company, 2023.

## ON THE WEB

# FACTSURFER

Factsurfer.com gives you a safe, fun way to find more information.

1. Go to www.factsurfer.com.
2. Enter "hovercraft" into the search box and click 🔍.
3. Select your book cover to see a list of related content.

# Index



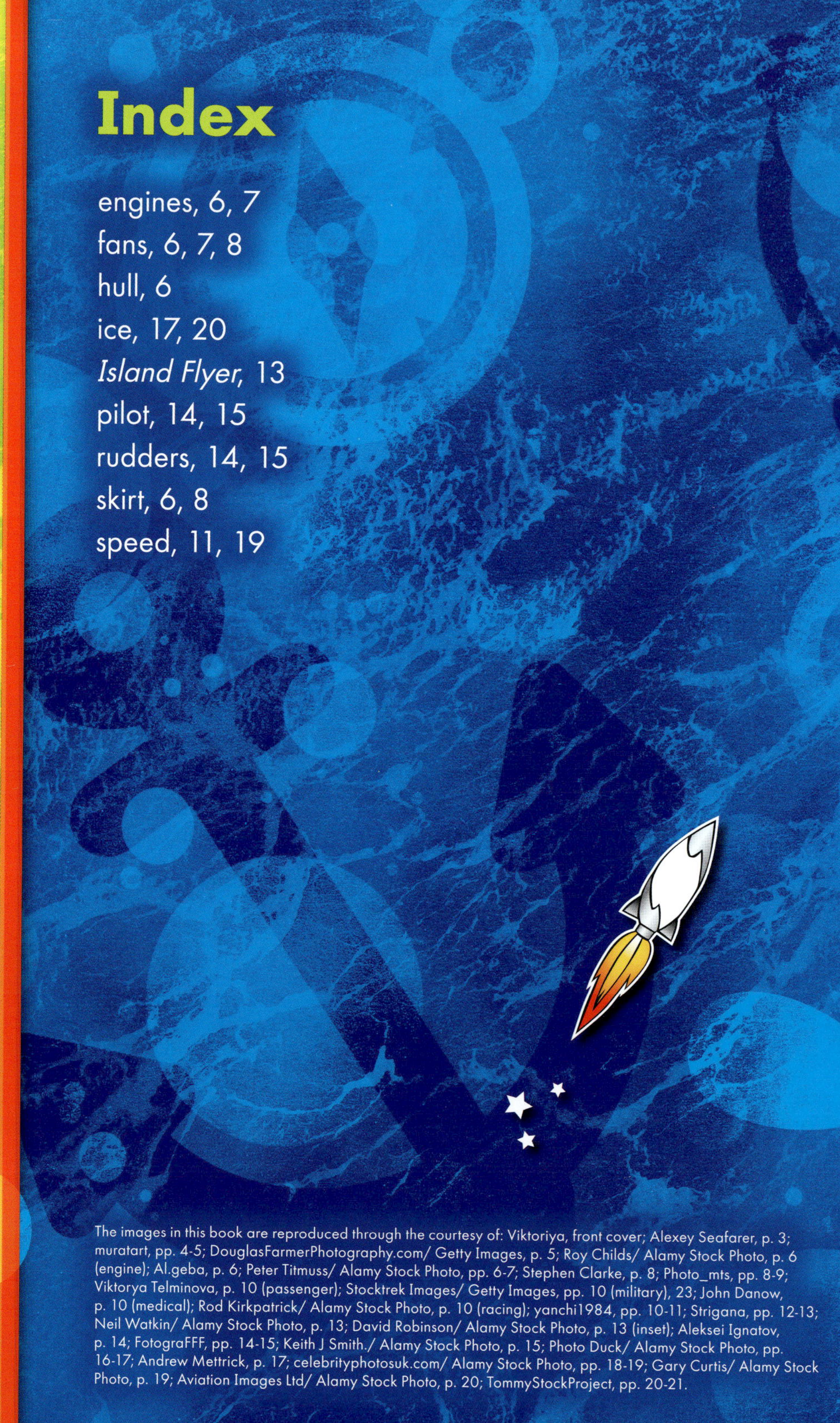

The images in this book are reproduced through the courtesy of: Viktoriya, front cover; Alexey Seafarer, p. 3; muratart, pp. 4-5; DouglasFarmerPhotography.com/ Getty Images, p. 5; Roy Childs/ Alamy Stock Photo, p. 6 (engine); Al.geba, p. 6; Peter Titmuss/ Alamy Stock Photo, pp. 6-7; Stephen Clarke, p. 8; Photo_mts, pp. 8-9; Viktorya Telminova, p. 10 (passenger); Stocktrek Images/ Getty Images, pp. 10 (military), 23; John Danow, p. 10 (medical); Rod Kirkpatrick/ Alamy Stock Photo, p. 10 (racing); yanchi1984, pp. 10-11; Strigana, pp. 12-13; Neil Watkin/ Alamy Stock Photo, p. 13; David Robinson/ Alamy Stock Photo, p. 13 (inset); Aleksei Ignatov, p. 14; FotograFFF, pp. 14-15; Keith J Smith./ Alamy Stock Photo, p. 15; Photo Duck/ Alamy Stock Photo, pp. 16-17; Andrew Mettrick, p. 17; celebrityphotosuk.com/ Alamy Stock Photo, pp. 18-19; Gary Curtis/ Alamy Stock Photo, p. 19; Aviation Images Ltd/ Alamy Stock Photo, p. 20; TommyStockProject, pp. 20-21.